MONTANA

MONTANA

HELLO
U.S.A.

by Rita LaDoux

 Lerner Publications Company

You'll find this picture of a bitterroot flower at the beginning of each chapter in this book. Bitterroot is Montana's state flower. It grows best in areas with lots of sunshine, and it blooms in late June. Explorer Meriwether Lewis gave bitterroot its scientific name (Lewisia rediviva) *while exploring the Montana region.*

Cover (left): Grinnell Lake in Glacier National Park. Cover (right): Grizzly bear cub. Pages 2–3: Herding cattle near White Sulphur Springs. Page 3: Skier jumping at Big Mountain Ski Resort near Missoula.

This book is available in two editions:
Library binding by Lerner Publications Company, a division of Lerner Publishing Group
Soft cover by First Avenue Editions, an imprint of Lerner Publishing Group
241 First Avenue North
Minneapolis, MN 55401 U.S.A.

Website address: www.lernerbooks.com

Library of Congress Cataloging-in-Publication Data

LaDoux, Rita, 1951–
    Montana / by Rita LaDoux (Rev. and expanded 2nd ed.)
      p.   cm. — (Hello U.S.A.)
    Includes index.
    Summary: Introduces the geography, history, people, economy, and some of the
       state symbols of Montana.
    ISBN: 0–8225–4092–4 (lib. bdg. : alk paper)
    ISBN: 0–8225–0785–4 (pbk. : alk paper)
    1. Montana—Juvenile literature. [1. Montana.] I. Title. II. Series.
    F731.3.L34 2003
    978.6—dc21   2002003595

Manufactured in the United States of America
1 2 3 4 5 6 – JR – 08 07 06 05 04 03

CONTENTS

Autumn brings patches of color to the Rocky Mountains in Glacier National Park.

THE LAND

The Treasure State

ontana, which means "mountain" in Spanish, is many things to many people. Whether you call it the Land of Shining Mountains, the Treasure State, or the Big Sky Country, Montana is beautiful—and big. In fact, it is the fourth largest state in the country.

Stretching across the northwestern United States, Montana is a neighbor of Canada, North Dakota, South Dakota, Wyoming, and Idaho. Along Montana's northwestern boundary lies Glacier National Park. Yellowstone National Park cuts into Montana's southwestern corner.

A snowboarder snakes down Big Mountain. Snow covers some peaks in Montana 10 months of the year.

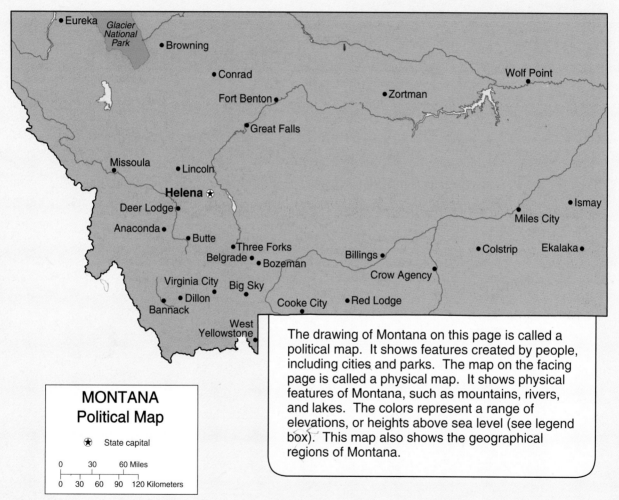

Eureka

Glacier National Park

Browning

Conrad

Fort Benton

Great Falls

Zortman

Wolf Point

Missoula

Lincoln

Helena ✪

Deer Lodge

Anaconda

Butte

Three Forks

Belgrade

Bozeman

Billings

Ismay

Miles City

Colstrip

Ekalaka

Crow Agency

Virginia City

Big Sky

Dillon

Cooke City

Red Lodge

Bannack

West Yellowstone

The drawing of Montana on this page is called a political map. It shows features created by people, including cities and parks. The map on the facing page is called a physical map. It shows physical features of Montana, such as mountains, rivers, and lakes. The colors represent a range of elevations, or heights above sea level (see legend box). This map also shows the geographical regions of Montana.

MONTANA
Political Map

✪ State capital

0   30   60 Miles

0   30   60   90   120 Kilometers

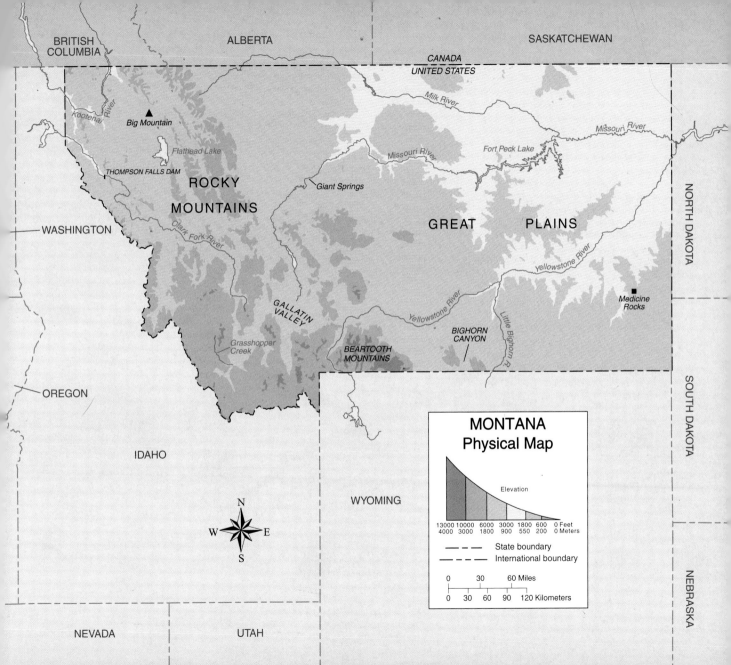

BRITISH COLUMBIA

ALBERTA

SASKATCHEWAN

CANADA
UNITED STATES

Kootenai River

▲ Big Mountain

Milk River

Missouri River

Flathead Lake

Missouri River

Fort Peck Lake

THOMPSON FALLS DAM

ROCKY

MOUNTAINS

Giant Springs

GREAT

PLAINS

NORTH DAKOTA

WASHINGTON

Clark Fork River

Yellowstone River

Medicine
Rocks

GALLATIN
VALLEY

Yellowstone River

OREGON

*Grasshopper
Creek*

BEARTOOTH
MOUNTAINS

BIGHORN
CANYON

Little Bighorn R.

SOUTH DAKOTA

IDAHO

MONTANA
Physical Map

WYOMING

Elevation

13000 10000 6000 3000 1800 600 0 Feet
4000 3000 1800 900 550 200 0 Meters

N
W — E
S

— — — State boundary
— — — International boundary

0   30   60 Miles

0   30   60   90   120 Kilometers

NEVADA

UTAH

NEBRASKA

Buffalo graze on the lightly snow-covered Great Plains in Montana. The plains rise to meet the Rocky Mountains in the distance.

The state has two geographic regions, the Great Plains and the Rocky Mountains. Montana's Great Plains roll across the eastern two-thirds of the state. This grass-covered region is mostly flat.

Millions of years ago, dinosaurs lumbered through swamps that flooded a large part of the Great Plains.

As the plants and animals in the swamps died, they sank to the bottom. The thick layer of decayed plants and animals was later buried by rock. Over thousands of years, the weight of the rock pressed the decayed layer into coal, one of Montana's most valuable minerals.

The Rocky Mountains region covers the western third of Montana. This area of the state contains a small section of the Rocky Mountains, a chain that stretches from Alaska to Mexico. Within Montana's Rockies are more than 50 smaller groups of mountains, called ranges.

The Rocky Mountains were formed millions of years ago when strong pressures in the earth's crust caused western North America to buckle. Enormous blocks of rock were lifted into tall ranges. Lava, or hot liquid rock, bubbled up to the surface from deep inside the earth. The lava cooled into solid rock, some of which contained copper and gold. Later, glaciers—huge, thick sheets of slow-moving ice—carved out the peaks and valleys of the Rockies.

Bighorn Canyon in southeastern Montana was carved by the swift current of the Bighorn River over millions of years. A dam built on the river tamed the rushing waters to create Bighorn Lake.

When rain falls on the western side of the Rockies, it collects in the Kootenai and Clark Fork Rivers and flows toward the Pacific. Rain that falls on the eastern slopes of the Rockies pours into the Milk, Missouri, and Yellowstone Rivers, which cut wide valleys as they wind eastward across the state.

Besides its mighty rivers, Montana boasts Flathead Lake, the largest natural lake in the western United States. Nestled in the mountains of western Montana, Flathead was formed by glaciers, as were the many smaller lakes that dot Montana's mountain slopes.

Dams built along the Missouri and Kootenai Rivers created other large lakes, or **reservoirs,** including Fort Peck Lake. Water released from reservoirs is used to turn engines that produce electricity and for **irrigation** to water crops.

The Clark Fork River roars through the Thompson Falls Dam in western Montana.

Montana has a lot of water, but some of the state gets only a little **precipitation** (rain and snow). More than 32 inches of precipitation usually fall on the western slopes of the Rockies each year. But the eastern mountains and plains are much drier, receiving about 13 inches per year.

In the western mountains, summers are cool and winters fairly warm. On the plains, however, summers can be scorching hot and winters bitterly cold. The state's highest temperature, recorded on the far eastern plains, was 117° F. The lowest temperature in winter was a bone-chilling −70° F.

Montana's climate supports a variety of wildflowers. Bear grass *(above left)* grows in meadows and open woods in the mountains. Pasqueflowers *(left)* bloom in early spring on bare hillsides.

A frost-covered buffalo roams a Montana wildlife preserve.

No matter what the season, the open plains cannot stop the ever-blowing winds. The wind blows through the grasses that cover the **prairies,** or grasslands, of the Great Plains. At one time, millions of buffalo ate the prairie grasses. Now the few buffalo left in Montana graze in wildlife preserves, where they are protected from hunters. Pronghorn antelope, mule deer, and prairie dogs rely on the grasslands for food and shelter.

Mountain goats perch on a ledge in Glacier National Park.

Grizzly bears, elks, moose, mountain goats, and bighorn sheep roam through Montana's mountains. The Rockies are forested with ash, birch, cedar, fir, pine, and spruce trees.

Booms and Busts

or centuries the people of Montana have had close ties to the land. Hunters, trappers, farmers, ranchers, miners, and loggers have made a living from the mountains and prairies of the state. Each group of people has its own story to tell. Twisted together like the strands of a rope, these stories tell the history of Montana.

Generations of Native Americans and European settlers have lived off of the land in Montana.

One story begins about 12,000 years ago with the first people to arrive in the land that would become Montana. These Native Americans may have walked to North America from Asia on a narrow strip of land that would later be called the Bering Strait land bridge. The Native Americans hunted buffalo and woolly mammoths, huge animals that looked like hairy elephants.

Over the next several thousand years, the world's climate changed drastically, and all the mammoths died. Hunters stalked smaller animals and gathered plants, berries, and roots to eat.

By 1600 the Native Americans had formed different groups. In the Rockies were the Flathead, Kootenai, and Kalispel Indians, who survived by hunting and fishing. The Blackfeet, Cheyenne, Crow, Assiniboine, and Gros Ventre hunted and farmed on the Great Plains.

Opposite page: This model of a woolly mammoth looks like the ones hunted by early Native Americans. The enormous animals were about 10 feet tall and weighed about 6 tons.

Plains Indians used a travois, or sled, to carry goods before they had horses.

The life of the Plains Indians changed when Spanish explorers brought horses to America. The Plains Indians had been living in villages so they could tend their farms. But in the 1600s, they began using horses. Many Indian groups quit farming and left their villages behind to follow and hunt roaming herds of buffalo.

Nearly everything the Plains Indians needed came from the buffalo. After a hunt, the women and older men skinned the buffalo and tanned the hides, which were used to make clothing and tepees. The Indians dried, roasted, or mixed the meat with berries and fat so that it wouldn't spoil. They carved buffalo bones into tools. And they used dried buffalo chips, or droppings, to fuel fires for cooking.

The hides and bones of buffalo provided materials for many of the Plains Indians' clothes, weapons, and tools.

Almost all of modern-day Montana was included in the Louisiana Purchase.

In 1682 France claimed a huge tract of land in North America that included most of what later became Montana. But Europeans did not come to the region until 1803, when France sold the territory, called Louisiana, to the United States in a deal called the Louisiana Purchase.

Eager to find out what his country had bought, U.S. president Thomas Jefferson sent explorers Meriwether Lewis and William Clark to map the new territory in 1804. Leaving from Saint Louis, Missouri, the expedition traveled about 1,600 miles up the Missouri River to the area that became Montana.

In Montana, Lewis and Clark paddled canoes along the Missouri River to Three Forks, at the base of the Rocky Mountains. There they traded their canoes to Indians for horses and rode across the mountains.

While in Montana, Lewis and Clark found many beavers. This discovery encouraged fur companies to build trading posts in the region. The soft, thick pelts of beavers were in demand in Europe because they could be made into stylish hats. The fur companies sent trappers called mountain men to the area. These men lived a rugged life, exploring wilderness known only to the Indians.

Fur companies employed mountain men to trap fur-bearing animals.

At trading posts set up by fur companies, mountain men gave Indians guns, alcohol, and tobacco in exchange for furs. In 1847 Montana's Fort Benton was built on the Missouri River. Steamboats loaded with trade goods were soon chugging up the river from Saint Louis, Missouri, to the fort. From this post, the boats headed back downstream filled with furs.

Indians and mountain men exchanged goods at trading posts.

Nellie Wibaux

Augusta Kohrs

Awbonnie Stuart

Montana's Frontierswomen

The women who helped to settle Montana in the 1800s came from many different backgrounds. Nellie Wibaux and her husband, Pierre, came from France. Their first Montana home was a log cabin with a sod roof that leaked during heavy rainstorms. Augusta Kohrs and her husband, Conrad, were of German ancestry. They built a successful cattle ranching business in western Montana. And Awbonnie Stuart, a Shoshone Indian, ranched for 26 years with her husband, Granville, and their 11 children.

Pioneer women in Montana worked hard. One day's chores might include making breakfast at 5:00 a.m., then sweeping and mopping the floors, making lunch, ironing, baking, tending the garden, mending clothes, preparing dinner, and doing the dishes.

White traders brought more than manufactured goods to the Indians. The traders exposed the Native Americans to European diseases such as smallpox and measles. Thousands of Indians died.

As Montana's Indian population was shrinking, waves of fortune seekers hit the region. In 1849 gold was discovered in California. Thousands of people from the eastern United States rushed west, hoping to make lots of money. But many of them found no gold in California, and they turned back to search the Rocky Mountains for the precious metal.

In 1862 prospectors discovered gold along Montana's Grasshopper Creek, and the Montana gold rush began. The gold rush brought not only settlers from east of the Mississippi River but also newcomers from other countries. Many people came from China, as well as Germany, France, Spain, and Sweden. Mining towns sprang up near gold strikes. Store owners charged high prices, and miners paid with gold dust.

The wealth also attracted outlaws, who stole from the miners, the stores, and the saloons. Prospectors

and townspeople captured and hanged the criminals. In 1864 the U.S. government helped restore order by making Montana a territory of the United States. This meant that U.S. laws could be enforced in the area. The territory's capital was Bannack. Virginia City was the capital from 1865 until 1875, when Helena became the capital.

Hoping to find gold, miners used large pans to sift rocks and water from Montana's creeks.

Cattle ranchers followed the miners to Montana. In the 1860s, cowboys began driving large herds of longhorn cattle to Montana from as far away as Texas. The ranchers sold beef to the miners and grazed their cattle on the grasslands. Montana's beef cattle industry grew as more ranchers came to the area.

Cowboys brought large herds of cattle to Montana in the late 1800s.

Roping

A Montana cowboy of the 1800s was never far from his lariat, or lasso, which he hung from the saddle on his horse. On the range, a cowboy might use his lariat to pull a cow out of the mud or to capture a cow trying to escape from the herd.

Lariats were made of braided rawhide or twisted grass. The lariat had to be stiff enough so that when a cowboy sent it flying through the air the loop would stay flat and open. A lariat also had to be very strong so a big cow, which might weigh as much as 1,200 pounds, couldn't break it.

A typical lariat was about 40 feet long. At one end of the lariat was a little loop called a honda. The main line of the lariat passed through the honda to form a big loop. To throw a lariat took great skill. The cowboy took the big loop and the main line in his throwing hand and held the rest of the lariat in his other hand. To steer his horse, the cowboy used the last two fingers of his nonthrowing hand to pull on the reins.

Railroad companies sent crews to slaughter buffalo in Montana and other western states.

Cattle ranchers and other settlers lived and worked on land that had been the home of Indians. The U.S. government signed **treaties** promising the Indians that some land would be saved for them. But the government did not keep its promises.

Instead, the government took back land it had assigned to the tribes and gave the land to settlers and railroad companies. Cattle ranchers, train crews, and sport hunters killed millions of buffalo—the Indians' main source of food.

Gradually the U.S. government forced most Indians in Montana onto **reservations**—areas of land reserved for Native Americans. The Indians were expected to give up hunting and to farm their land.

The Cree people did not have a reservation of their own for many years. Without land, they suffered many hardships. Finally, the Rocky Boy's Reservation was established in north central Montana. Little Bear, a Cree chief, stands in the middle of this photo.

Some Plains Indians fought hard to keep their land. One of their most famous struggles was the Battle of the Little Bighorn. In 1876 Sioux leaders Sitting Bull and Crazy Horse gathered almost 2,000 warriors from the Sioux, Cheyenne, and Arapaho tribes. The U.S. Army planned to attack the warriors while they were camped along the Little Bighorn River in Montana.

The way two artists drew the Battle of the Little Bighorn differs greatly. One artist showed Custer heroically leading his men into battle *(right)*. A Sioux artist drew pictures of dead U.S. Army soldiers after the Indians' victory *(opposite page)*.

    Before all the U.S. troops had arrived, Lieutenant
Colonel George Armstrong Custer led his army unit
in an attack on the Indians. During the short battle
that followed, Custer and his 264 soldiers were killed.

    The Plains Indians won the Battle of the Little
Bighorn, but they lost many other battles. Within a
few years after their victory, the Indians in Montana
had moved onto reservations. A new chapter in
Montana's history had begun.

During the 1880s, some settlers in the Territory of Montana were growing rich from the region's minerals. After silver and copper were discovered in Butte Hill, the hill became known as the Richest Hill on Earth.

Marcus Daly, a miner, became wealthy after finding copper in the mines of Anaconda and Butte Hill. Most miners were not interested in copper, but Daly and a few others understood its value. Miles and miles of copper wire were needed in the eastern United States for telephone and electric lines. Daly was determined to supply it.

Daly built the town of Anaconda around his mines. He wanted to make it Montana's capital. But a rival mine owner, William A. Clark, opposed his plan, and Helena remained Montana's capital. Daly and Clark were known as the Copper Kings. They continued their feud until Daly's death in 1900.

Railroads made the wealth of the Copper Kings possible. Trains hauled copper and other minerals east for sale and returned with mining machinery. The railroads also carried the state's wheat and cattle to market. People rode trains to Montana to settle on ranches and farms.

Towns sprang up along the railroad tracks. By the late 1880s, Montana's population had reached almost 150,000. Many people had decided to make Montana their home, and in 1889 the U.S. government admitted Montana to the Union, making it the 41st state.

Many trains were fueled by coal from Montana.

During the early 1900s, more and more settlers came to Montana, attracted by the railroads' promises of good farmland. Many tourists started to visit Montana after Glacier National Park was created in 1910.

Trains, the best mode of transportation at the turn of the century, were fueled by coal, which Montana had in abundance. In 1924 mining companies came to the town of Colstrip. Using heavy machinery, workers stripped away trees and soil to uncover coal.

Montanans profited from mining coal until the Great Depression of the 1930s. During this slump in the nation's economy, many people had little or no money to buy food and other necessities. As a result, factories around the United States made fewer goods or stopped manufacturing altogether.

The 1930s brought natural disasters to Montana. A plague of grasshoppers ruined crops, forcing people to leave the state. In some areas, whole towns—homes, farms, and schools—were abandoned.

Factories also bought less coal and other raw materials needed to make goods. With few buyers for their products, miners and loggers lost their jobs. At the same time, hot, dry weather scorched the plains. Crops and cattle died for lack of water. Farmers and ranchers abandoned their land.

Cattle ranching has been an important Montana industry since the late 1800s.

Montana began to recover from its slump when World War II started in 1939. The U.S. government needed beef from the state's cattle ranches to feed

soldiers. Factories demanded copper and coal from Montana's mines to build weapons and to fuel factories.

After the war ended in 1945, Montana's wealth grew. Oil was found in the state in the 1950s. Around this time, tourism became a major industry in Montana. Visitors came to the state's parks, historic sites, dude ranches, and ski resorts. Montana's natural beauty and opportunities for outdoor recreation—hiking, skiing, fishing, and other sports—held great appeal for people seeking a change from city life.

During the 1970s, the United States faced an energy shortage. Montana's resources were in great demand. Tons of coal were mined and sold. Coal mining near Colstrip expanded. The state's oil production also increased.

Montanans faced hard times in the 1980s. Fuel prices fell, and many miners lost their jobs. Montana's lumber industry declined. A drought hit the state, causing problems for farmers and their crops.

Montana's state lawmakers meet at the capitol building in the city of Helena.

But by the 1990s, farming had become profitable again. New industries such as construction and manufacturing developed. Cities like Missoula, Bozeman, and Belgrade began growing rapidly. And tourists seeking the peace and quiet or the adventure of Montana's wilderness kept coming to the state.

From the Indians to the miners, many strands have already been wound into Montana's history. Modern Montanans continue to add their stories to the history of the state.

PEOPLE & ECONOMY

Life under the Big Sky

laska, Texas, and California are the only states larger than Montana, yet the Big Sky Country has fewer people than Rhode Island, the nation's smallest state. Most of Montana's 902,000 residents live in the Rocky Mountains region or in the river valleys of the Great Plains, where many miles separate ranches and towns.

Montana's small population creates problems for such a large state. Keeping miles and miles of roads in good repair is expensive. The tax money taken from the state's few residents must pay for those roads, for schools, and for other public services.

Providing a good education for students in rural areas is difficult. Many students attend city schools. But children who live on ranches and farms sometimes share their classrooms with only a few other students. These schools usually cannot afford to offer many different classes or to buy computers.

Some students who live in rural areas *(opposite page)* attend one-room schools *(above)*.

Slightly more than half of Montana's people live in cities or large towns. Most of Montana's towns grew from small mining camps or railroad stops. The largest cities are Billings, Missoula, Great Falls, Butte, Bozeman, and Helena, the state capital. Billings, the largest of these cities, has about 90,000 people.

Indians were the only residents of Montana until the 1800s, but they now make up about 6 percent of the state's population. Seven reservations are home to most of the 56,000 Native Americans living in Montana.

The big city is far away from many Montanans' homes.

Cowboys display their team roping skills at a Crow Agency rodeo *(left)*. A German-Scot weaver demonstrates her craft at Red Lodge *(below)*.

About 90 percent of Montanans are white people. Many of their grandparents came from midwestern or southern states. Others have ancestors from European countries such as Norway, Sweden, Finland, Wales, Ireland, and Germany. About 2 percent of Montanans are Latino. The remaining Montanans are Asian or African American.

The state's European, Native American, and other cultures are represented in community events. Performers dance to German polkas at the Festival of Nations at Red Lodge in south central Montana. Indian dancers whirl trailing feathers at powwows in the towns of Browning and Crow Agency. Cowboys test their skills at rodeos such as the annual Bucking Horse Sale in Miles City.

Little Bighorn Battlefield National Monument reminds visitors of the historic battle in southern Montana.

Every year, millions of people travel to Montana. At Little Bighorn Battlefield National Monument, tourists explore the battlegrounds of the Little Bighorn. The Grant-Kohrs Ranch gives visitors an idea of what life was like for early cattle ranchers. On the prairie, vacationers can ride horses along trails or take covered-wagon trips.

One of the most scenic of Montana's tourist attractions is Glacier National Park. Backpackers and mountain climbers enjoy climbing Glacier's rugged mountain peaks. Skiers speed down Montana's snow-packed mountain slopes. Rafters splash through river rapids, and fishers cast for trout in the cold mountain streams that make Montana an excellent place for fly-fishing.

Many Montanans help tourists enjoy their stay in the state. They work in what are called service jobs, helping people or businesses. The people who load railroad cars in Billings and Great Falls also have service jobs. Other service workers include doctors, salesclerks, truck drivers, and mechanics. More Montanans work in services than in any other field.

Montana visitors can admire the steep peaks and swift rivers of Glacier National Park.

The government employs 16 percent of Montanans. Government workers include rangers at state and national parks, teachers, and police officers.

Manufacturing employs 6 percent of working Montanans. Many of the state's factories produce lumber and wood products. After cutting down trees from Montana's forests, loggers send the timber to sawmills where it is cut into boards. Factory workers in Missoula process some of the lumber into plywood or paper.

Trucks bring logs cut from Montana's forests to sawmills and factories.

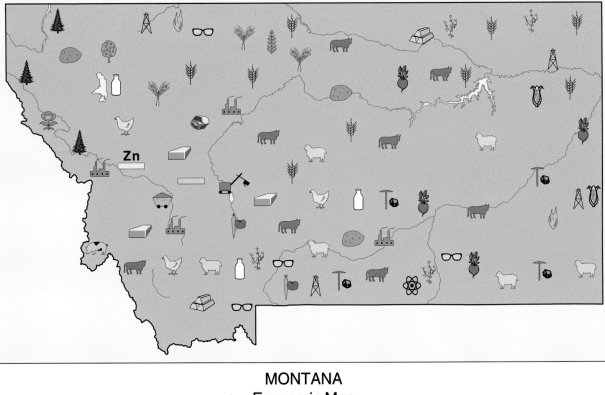

MONTANA
Economic Map

The symbols on this map show where different economic activities take place in Montana. The legend below explains what each symbol stands for.

						Tourism
Barley	Corn	Granite	Manufacturing	Oats	Rye	Uranium
Beef cattle	Forest products	Hogs	Milk	Oil	Sheep	Vegetables
Coal	Fruit	Iron ore	Natural gas	Potatoes	Silver	Wheat
Copper	Gold	Lead	Nursery products	Poultry	Sugar beets	**Zn** Zinc

Other factories make food products or process minerals. Some food-processing plants refine sugar or mill flour. Using resources mined in Montana, some of the state's workers make metal pipe, mold bricks, and mix cement. Workers in Billings refine the state's oil.

Montana earns a lot of money from its oil wells.

Most of the minerals unearthed in Montana are sold to factories in other states. Oil and coal, two major sources of fuel, are Montana's most valuable minerals. Eastern Montana has some of the largest coal reserves in the United States. Miners also dig copper, silver, gold, and lead, primarily from southwestern Montana. The state is a major producer of these metals.

Agriculture earns only 4 percent of the state's money. About one-third of Montana's farmland is used to grow crops. Because of the state's dry climate, farmers must

Farmers in Montana grow cherries and other crops.

irrigate some of this land. Wheat and barley are the state's main crops, but farmers also plant hay, potatoes, sugar beets, and cherry trees. Plump, delicious berries—strawberries, raspberries, blackberries, and huckleberries—grow in many parts of Montana. A large number of Christmas trees grow on farms in the Rocky Mountains, and the town of Eureka claims to be the Christmas Tree Capital of the World.

Montana ranchers raise livestock such as sheep *(below)* and cattle *(right)*.

Cattle ranchers still play a part in Montana's agriculture. Beef and dairy cattle and sheep graze on about two-thirds of the state's farmland. Hogs are also raised. The broad, open ranges, scattered with cattle and cowboys and cowgirls, keep the spirit of Montana's first ranchers alive.

THE ENVIRONMENT

Cleaning Up the Mines

ontana's wealth lies in its natural resources—timbered mountains, grass-covered prairies, minerals such as coal and gold, and breathtaking scenery. Many Montanans depend on these natural resources to make a living. But when some valuable resources are used, other equally valuable resources are threatened.

For example, minerals have brought money, jobs, and people to Montana. But mining these resources has damaged Montana's land, water, and wildlife.

To unearth metals such as gold and copper, which are hidden in underground rocks, miners blast or dig a huge, gaping hole out of the land to create an **open-pit mine.** Miners then remove rock from the mine and separate the metals from the rock.

Open-pit mines can damage Montana's land, water, and wildlife.

By creating an open-pit mine, people destroy the area's trees and grasses. People also uncover loose soil and rocks that produce acid, a harmful sour chemical. Rainwater washes the dirt and acid into nearby streams and rivers, clouding the waterways and poisoning fish and plants.

In the gold-rush days, miners used mercury to separate gold from lead rocks. The miners left behind piles of lead and mercury, which are toxic, or poisonous, metals. These wastes seeped into both surface water and **groundwater**—water below the earth's surface that is used for drinking.

Miners no longer use mercury, but new methods of mining can be just as dangerous. Gold miners crush rocks containing small amounts of gold and then wash the rocks with cyanide. Cyanide pulls the gold from the rock. This process is called heap leaching.

Miners keep the cyanide, a highly poisonous chemical, in a pond lined with watertight plastic. But the cyanide sometimes leaks out of the pond and into groundwater. People who drink the contaminated groundwater can be poisoned.

Even if the pond doesn't leak, it is dangerous. Thirsty birds and animals see the cyanide pond and think that it holds water, not toxic chemicals. Thousands of birds have been poisoned by drinking from cyanide ponds.

Heap Leaching

1. Ore containing gold is mined and then crushed.
2. Ore is spread out in a heap, and a cyanide solution is sprayed over the ore. Waterproof liners under the heap and the pond help prevent the solution from leaking into the ground.
3. Cyanide solution and gold trickle to the bottom of the heap. Then they are pumped to a processing plant.
4. At the processing plant, the gold is recovered from the solution.
5. The solution goes to the tank to be used again.

Montanans are working with the mining industry to protect people and animals from cyanide. For example, mining companies have started putting nets over some cyanide ponds so that birds won't land there. And in 1998 Montana voters approved a law that bans the development of new open-pit mines that practice heap leaching with cyanide.

Since the 1970s, Montana's legislature has passed laws that require mining companies to clean up their waste. This is done through a process called **reclamation.** Montana requires companies to create a plan for reclamation before they begin mining. For example, coal miners must rebuild the land after they have dug all the coal from a site. And gold miners must carefully collect their cyanide and dispose of it safely.

To separate gold from rock, miners sometimes use sprinklers *(top)* loaded with toxic chemicals. When the site is no longer in use, the land is reclaimed *(bottom)*.

State laws have helped to protect Montana's landscape from further damage, but old abandoned mines and open-pit mines are still a potential source of pollution. More than 3,800 abandoned mines exist.

Reclaiming old mines is expensive. Mining companies sometimes pay for the process, but often it is too costly. Then the government must pay to reclaim the mines. A state agency called the Mine Waste Cleanup Bureau tries to reclaim old mines, but the project is huge. So some mines are left open, exposing loose soil and acidic rocks for years.

State workers hope to reclaim this abandoned mine in Zortman, Montana.

As the dangers of careless mining become clear, more mining companies are cleaning up after themselves. Some miners refill open pits with the earth taken out earlier and then plant trees and grasses.

Even Montanans who aren't miners can help protect their state's resources. Reporting signs of polluted water, such as dead fish or bad-tasting drinking water, is one way to help. Asking the government to pass laws to reclaim open-pit mines is another way to help. Montanans can make sure that the wealth and beauty of their state is protected.

Montanans take pride in the beauty of their state, and many residents are working to preserve it.

ALL ABOUT MONTANA

Fun Facts

So many dinosaur bones have been found near Ekalaka, Montana, that the town has been nicknamed Skeleton Flats.

Montana's Roe River, the world's shortest river, travels only 201 feet—less than the length of a football field. The Roe flows out of Montana's Giant Springs, a large freshwater pool, and into the Missouri River.

At Medicine Rocks in eastern Montana, Indian hunters once called on magical spirits to help them catch more buffalo.

In 1993 the town of Ismay, Montana, changed its name to Joe, Montana, in honor of football star Joe Montana.

Last Chance Gulch, the main street in Helena, Montana, was once a gold-mining area. The valley got its name in 1864, when some miners stopped there for one last chance to find gold. They struck it big—mines in the area soon produced over $20 million in gold!

Montana did not have a daytime speed limit on its roads from 1995 to 1999. Drivers could go as fast as they wanted during the day as long as they were careful. In 1999 the government enforced a speed limit. Drivers on the state's highways must drive between 65 and 75 miles per hour.

Last Chance Gulch

STATE SONG

Montana's state song was written at a party in Helena in 1910. It was performed publicly two days later. The governor liked the song so much he declared it to be Montana's state song. State lawmakers officially adopted it in 1945.

MONTANA

Music by Joseph E. Howard; words by Charles C. Cohan

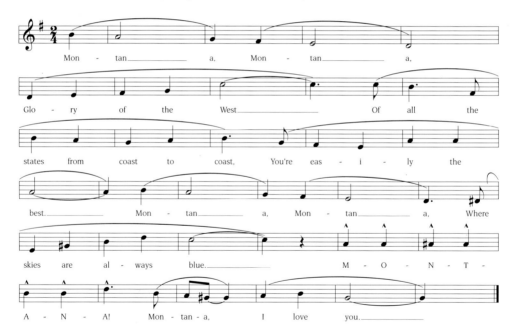

You can hear "Montana" by visiting this website:
<http://www.50states.com/songs/mont.htm>

A MONTANA RECIPE

Huckleberries are wild berries that look a lot like blueberries. They grow throughout Montana's mountains. This recipe calls for huckleberry preserves. If you can't find huckleberry preserves in your local grocery store, substitute another Montana product—raspberry or strawberry preserves.

HUCKLEBERRY BARS

You will need:

¾ cup butter
1 cup brown sugar
1½ cups flour
½ teaspoon salt

½ teaspoon baking soda
1½ cups oatmeal
1 jar (9 ounces) huckleberry preserves

1. Ask an adult to preheat oven to 400° F.
2. Using electric mixer, cream butter and sugar.
3. Add rest of ingredients, except huckleberry preserves. Mix together until crumbly.
4. Pat half of crumb mixture into bottom of 9 x 13 inch pan.
5. Spread preserves on top. Then sprinkle with rest of crumb mixture.
6. Bake for 25 minutes.

HISTORICAL TIMELINE

10,000 B.C.   Native Americans hunt mammoths in what would later become Montana.

A.D. 1600s   Plains Indians begin to hunt on horseback.

1682   France claims a huge part of North America, including what would become Montana.

1804   Lewis and Clark begin exploring the area known as the Louisiana Purchase.

1847   Montana's Fort Benton is built.

1862   After gold is discovered along Grasshopper Creek, Montana's gold rush begins.

1864   The U.S. Congress establishes the Montana Territory.

1875   Helena becomes the capital of the Montana Territory.

1876   Plains Indians defeat the U.S. army at the Battle of the Little Bighorn.

1880s Miners such as William Clark and Marcus Daly grow rich from copper mining in Montana.

1889 Montana becomes the 41st state.

1910 Glacier National Park is created.

1924 Coal is mined at Colstrip, Montana.

1929 Montana's economy suffers with the start of the Great Depression.

1939–1945 Montana's beef, copper, coal, and other products contribute to the war efforts of the United States and its allies during World War II.

1951 Oil is discovered in Montana.

1998 Montanans vote to ban new open-pit mines that practice cyanide heap leaching.

2001 Montana's first female governor, Judy Martz, takes office.

OUTSTANDING MONTANANS

Dolly Smith Cusker Akers (1901–1986), who grew up in Wolf Point, Montana, was the first Assiniboine Indian woman to lead the Fort Peck tribal governing board. In 1932 Akers became the first woman and the first Indian to be elected to the Montana state legislature.

Dolly Smith Cusker Akers

John Bozeman (1835–1867) headed west with gold seekers in 1862. He blazed a trail that led directly to Montana's mining camps. The city of Bozeman, Montana, carries the explorer's name.

John Bozeman

Dana Carvey (born 1955) is a comedian who was born in Missoula, Montana. Carvey appeared on *Saturday Night Live* from 1986 until 1992, and he won an Emmy Award for his work. He has starred in *Wayne's World* and other comic films.

Chief Dull Knife (1810?–1883?), also known as Morning Star, was a leader of the Northern Cheyenne people. After the tribe was moved from Montana to a reservation in Oklahoma, Dull Knife helped his people return to their Montana hunting grounds. Indians on the Northern Cheyenne Reservation in Montana call themselves the Morning Star People in Dull Knife's honor.

Chief Dull Knife

Chief Plenty Coups (1849?–1932) helped the Crow Indians keep some of the land in Montana by carefully planning treaties with the U.S. government. Plenty Coups worked closely with white people but practiced the traditions of the Crow.

Chief Plenty Coups

William A. Clark (1839–1925) and **Marcus Daly** (1841–1900) are sometimes called the Copper Kings because both men became wealthy from their copper mines in Montana. Clark and Daly were also politically active.

William A. Clark

Gary Cooper (1901–1961) was once a guide in Yellowstone National Park but is more famous for his career as an actor. Born in Helena, Montana, Cooper appeared in more than 90 movies and won Academy Awards for his performances in *Sergeant York* and *High Noon.*

Richard Grant (1794–1862) set up the first ranch in Montana. Grant made a practice of trading one of his healthy cows for two tired and weak cows herded by pioneers traveling the Oregon Trail. Grant then fattened the weak cattle on Montana's rich pastures.

Gary Cooper

A. B. Guthrie Jr. (1901–1991) set many of his novels and stories in Montana, his home state. He also wrote many scripts for western films, including *Shane.* In 1950 Guthrie won a Pulitzer Prize for his book *The Way West.*

John R. (Jack) Horner (born 1946), a native of Shelby, Montana, found the first dinosaur nests ever uncovered. The nests held hundreds of dinosaur eggs and the bones of baby dinosaurs. Horner is the curator of paleontology at the Museum of the Rockies in Bozeman, Montana. He has also worked as a consultant for *Jurassic Park* and other movies about dinosaurs.

Marcus Daly

Chet Huntley (1911–1974) was born in Cardwell, Montana. He worked as a reporter for three major television networks—ABC, CBS, and NBC—before anchoring *The Huntley-Brinkley Report,* a nightly television news program.

A. B. Guthrie Jr.

Dorothy M. Johnson

Dorothy M. Johnson (1905–1984) grew up in Montana. Her books tell the history of the American West. The movies *The Man Who Shot Liberty Valance* and *A Man Called Horse* are based on Johnson's stories.

Yellowstone Kelly (1849–1928) led fur traders and pioneers through Montana. Born Luther Sage Kelly in New York, the guide was nicknamed Yellowstone because he was an expert scout in the Yellowstone River valley.

Myrna Loy

Evel Knievel (born 1938) is a daredevil famous for his motorcycle stunts. He has jumped over cars, buses, and the Grand Canyon, but not without breaking at least 35 bones. He was born Robert Knieval in Butte, Montana.

Myrna Loy (1905–1993) was nicknamed the Queen of Hollywood. The actress starred in more than 120 movies, including the *Thin Man* series and *The Best Years of Our Lives.* In 1991 Loy won an honorary Academy Award for career achievement. She was born in Radersburg, Montana.

Michael J. Mansfield (1903–2001), raised in Great Falls, Montana, was a miner, college professor, and politician. He served for many years in the U.S. House of Representatives and in the U.S. Senate. From 1977 to 1988, Mansfield was the U.S. ambassador to Japan.

Michael J. Mansfield

Dave McNally (born 1942), a baseball player from Billings, Montana, pitched for the Baltimore Orioles during the 1960s and 1970s. During his career, McNally helped the Orioles win 184 games. In 1970 he became the first pitcher to hit a grand slam in the World Series. McNally retired from baseball in 1975.

Dave McNally

James E. Murray (1876–1961) represented Montana in the U.S. Senate from 1934 until 1961. The Democrat served longer than any other senator from Montana. Murray worked to help U.S. workers, to set up a national health insurance plan, and to create dams on the Missouri River. Born in Canada, he lived most of his life in Butte, Montana.

Jeannette Rankin (1880–1973), born in Missoula, Montana, was the first woman elected to the U.S. Congress. Rankin worked to get government funds to help support poor women and their children.

Jeannette Rankin

Martha Raye (1916–1994), born in Butte, Montana, was a television, film, and stage star. Her film credits include *The Boys from Syracuse, Monsieur Verdoux,* and *Pufnstuf.* In 1968 the Academy of Motion Picture Arts and Sciences presented Raye with the Jean Hersholt Humanitarian Award for her work entertaining United States troops overseas.

Martha Raye

Charles Marion Russell (1865–1926) worked as a hunter and a cowboy in the Territory of Montana before becoming a full-time artist. Russell's drawings, paintings, and sculptures capture the spirit of life on the western frontier.

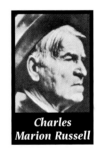
Charles Marion Russell

Granville Stuart (1834–1918) was one of the first miners to discover gold in Montana, but his main interest was raising cattle. Stuart was involved in Montana politics and spent his later years writing about the state's history.

Robert Yellowtail (1889–1988) became the first Indian superintendent of the Crow Indian Reservation in 1934. Under his leadership, which lasted for 50 years, the Crow Indians managed reservation affairs for the first time.

Granville Stuart

FACTS-AT-A-GLANCE

Nickname: Treasure State

Song: "Montana"

Motto: *Oro y Plata* (Gold and Silver)

Flower: bitterroot

Tree: ponderosa pine

Bird: western meadowlark

Animal: grizzly bear

Fish: blackspotted cutthroat trout

Butterfly: mourning cloak

Grass: bluebunch wheatgrass

Date and ranking of statehood:
    November 8, 1889, the 41st state

Capital: Helena

Area: 145,556 square miles

Rank in area, nationwide: 4th

Average January temperature: 18° F

Average July temperature: 68° F

Montana's flag became official in 1981. It contains the state seal, which shows the mountain scenery that gave the state its name.

POPULATION GROWTH

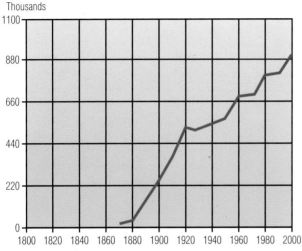

Thousands

This chart shows how Montana's population has grown from 1870 to 2000.

Montana's state seal was designed in 1865, before Montana was a state. It shows the state's scenery and important industries—mining and farming.

Population: 902,195 (2000 census)

Rank in population, nationwide: 44th

Major cities and populations: (2000 census)
Billings (89,847), Missoula (57,053), Great Falls (56,690), Butte-Silver Bow (34,606), Bozeman (27,509), Helena (25,780)

U.S. senators: 2

U.S. representatives: 1

Electoral votes: 3

Natural resources: coal, copper, gold, lead, natural gas, oil, sand and gravel, silver, soil, trees

Agricultural products: barley, beef, blackberries, cherries, hay, huckleberries, milk, potatoes, raspberries, strawberries, sugar beets, wheat

Manufactured goods: clay and glass products, food products, lumber and wood products, petroleum and coal products, printed materials

WHERE MONTANANS WORK

Services—64 percent (services include jobs in trade; community, social, and personal services; finance, insurance, and real estate; transportation, communication, and utilities)

Government—16 percent

Agriculture—7 percent

Manufacturing—6 percent

Construction—6 percent

Mining—1 percent

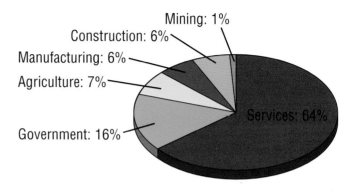

GROSS STATE PRODUCT

Services—62 percent

Government—16 percent

Manufacturing—8 percent

Construction—5 percent

Mining—5 percent

Agriculture—4 percent

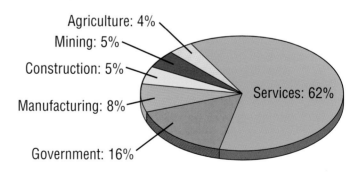

MONTANA WILDLIFE

Mammals: badger, beaver, bighorn sheep, buffalo, coyote, elk, grizzly bear, mink, moose, mountain goat, mountain sheep, mule deer, muskrat, prairie dog, pronghorn antelope, wolf

Birds: bald eagle, duck, hawk, goose, grouse, osprey, partridge, pheasant, trumpeter swan

Reptiles and amphibians: bull snake, Columbia spotted frog, garter snakes, long-toed salamander, milk snake, Pacific chorus frog, racer, rattlesnakes, rubber boa, tailed frog, western hognose snake, western toad

Fish: channel catfish, cutthroat trout, grayling, lake trout, northern pike, paddlefish, perch, rainbow trout, salmon, walleye

Trees: alder, ash, aspen, birch, cedar, fir, juniper, larch, pine, spruce

Wild plants: aster, bitterroot, columbine, daisy, dryad, lily, lupine, poppy, primrose, wild grasses

A coyote spies its next meal on a snowy Montana hillside.

PLACES TO VISIT

Beartooth Scenic Byway, between Red Lodge and Cooke City
The highway through the Beartooth Mountains climbs to Beartooth Pass, 10,947 feet above sea level, where there's snow year round. Enjoy the mountain wildlife and spectacular views.

Big Sky Resort, southwestern Montana
The mountains around the Gallatin Valley near Bozeman get about 400 inches of snow each year. In the winter, downhill skiers and other sports lovers flock to Big Sky to take advantage of the snow. In the summer, opportunities abound for hikers, horseback riders, fishers, and whitewater rafters.

C. M. Russell Museum, Great Falls
This museum houses the world's largest collection of the works of western artist Charles M. Russell. The works of other western artists are also on display.

Glacier National Park, northwestern Montana
This large area of wilderness includes more than 50 glaciers and has plenty to do for explorers. The park has more than 200 lakes and streams, and more than 730 miles of hiking trails. Visitors can also drive along the scenic Going-to-the-Sun Road.

Grant-Kohrs Ranch National Historic Site, Deer Lodge
Once the headquarters of a 10-million-acre cattle ranch, the site covers 1,500 acres. Established in the 1860s, the ranch explores the history of cowboys and ranchers. The house and grounds of the ranch have been restored to their original appearance.

Lewis & Clark National Historic Trail

Retrace the steps of explorers Lewis and Clark in Montana on foot, by car, or by boat. An interpretive center in Great Falls provides more information about their journey.

Little Bighorn Battlefield National Monument, near Crow Agency

This is the site of Custer's Last Stand, where a group of Plains Indian warriors killed General Custer's soldiers to the last man in 1876. Visitors can tour the battlefield, a visitor center, and the nearby Custer National Cemetery.

Museum of the Rockies, Bozeman

This museum explores 4.6 billion years of the cultural and natural history of the northern Rocky Mountains. Exhibits teach visitors about dinosaurs and fossils found in the area. The museum also features a planetarium and a re-creation of a late 1800s Montana farm.

Virginia City, near Dillon

Virginia City was once the territorial capital of Montana and a gold boomtown. But after the gold ran out, the town froze in time. Visitors can explore late 1800s buildings, go to museums devoted to the area's history, and even pan for gold.

Yellowstone National Park, southwestern Montana

Montana is the gateway to the world's first national park. Most of Yellowstone is located in Wyoming, but three of the park's entrances are in Montana. See famous natural features like Old Faithful, Mammoth Hot Springs, and the Grand Canyon of the Yellowstone.

ANNUAL EVENTS

Race to the Sky, Lincoln—*February*

Bucking Horse Sale, Miles City—*May*

Whoop-up Trail Days, Conrad—*May*

Red Lodge Music Festival, Red Lodge—*June*

North American Indian Days, Browning—*July*

Wild Horse Stampede Rodeo, Wolf Point—*July*

Montana State Fair, Great Falls—*July–August*

Crow Fair and Rodeo, Crow Agency—*August*

Festival of Nations, Red Lodge—*August*

Winterbration, West Yellowstone—*December*

LEARN MORE ABOUT MONTANA

General

Fradin, Dennis Brindell, and Judith Bloom Fradin. *Montana.* New York: Children's Press, 1997.

George, Charles, and Linda George. *Montana.* New York: Children's Press, 2000. For older readers.

Special Interest

Berman, Ruth. *American Bison.* Minneapolis, MN: Carolrhoda Books, Inc., 1992. Text and photographs describe the history, life cycle, and physical features of the large animals that once roamed Montana.

Bowen, Andy Russell. *The Back of Beyond: A Story about Lewis and Clark.* Minneapolis, MN: Carolrhoda Books, Inc., 1997. This biography tells the story of the explorers' trek across the Louisiana Territory to the Pacific Ocean. Lewis and Clark followed the Missouri River through what later became Montana.

Meli, Franco. *A Day with a Cheyenne.* Minneapolis, MN: Runestone Press, 1999. Artwork and historical photos illustrate the history and culture of the Cheyenne Indians. Readers spend a day with Painted Shield, a fictional Cheyenne hunter who lived in what later became southeastern Montana during the late 1800s.

Patent, Dorothy Hinshaw. *In Search of the Maiasaurs.* New York: Benchmark Books, 1999. When paleontologists unearthed a large bed of dinosaur bones in northwestern Montana, they discovered a dinosaur called the maiasaur. These findings helped scientists learn more about how the dinosaurs lived and died.

Stein, R. Conrad. *The Battle of the Little Bighorn.* New York: Children's Press, 1997. A group of Plains Indians defeated and killed General George Custer and all of his soldiers at the Battle of the Little Bighorn in Montana. This book examines the battle and its causes.

Tarbescu, Edith. *The Crow.* New York: Franklin Watts, 2000. Looks at the Crow Indians' culture and history, including the Crow's role in the Battle of the Little Bighorn. Describes life on the Crow reservation in Montana.

Fiction

Corcoran, Barbara. *Wolf at the Door.* New York: Atheneum, 1993. For older readers. Life changes when Lee's family moves from Missoula to the Montana woods. Feeling overshadowed by her talented but pesky younger sister, Lee holds her own by protecting area wolves.

Crow, Joe Medicine. *Brave Wolf and the Thunderbird.* New York: Abbeville Press Publishers, 1998. This picture book describes what happens when the Thunderbird, a Crow spirit, asks Brave Wolf to protect her young from a monster.

Ferguson, Alane, and Gloria Skurzynski. *The Hunted*. Washington, D.C.: National Geographic Society, 2000. For older readers. Part of the National Parks Mystery series, this book is set in Glacier National Park. When the Landon family travels to Glacier to investigate the disappearance of grizzly bear cubs, young Jack and Ashley uncover another mystery.

WEBSITES

Discovering Montana
<http://www.discoveringmontana.com/css/default.asp>
Montana's official state website offers information about the state's government, agencies, services, schools, and businesses.

Montana Vacation, Adventure, Recreation, and Travel Planning Guide
<http://www.visitmt.com/>
Montana travelers can plan their vacations using this website. It features photos and helpful information about the state's parks, museums, ski areas, hiking trails, and more.

Montana Kids
<http://www.montanakids.com/home.htm>
Just for kids, this colorful site provides fun facts about Montana wildlife, businesses, history, places to visit, and activities. Kids can also play the site's Montana-themed games.

PRONUNCIATION GUIDE

Anaconda (an-uh-KAHN-duh)

Arapaho (uh-RAP-uh-hoh)

Assiniboine (uh-SIHN-uh-boyn)

Butte (BYOOT)

Cheyenne (shy-AN)

Gros Ventre (GROH vahnt)

Helena (HEHL-uh-nuh)

Kalispel (KAL-uh-spehl)

Kootenai (KOOT-ihn-ay)

Missoula (muh-ZOO-luh)

Sioux (SOO)

Flowers known as little sunflowers add color to Montana's wilderness.

GLOSSARY

groundwater: water that lies beneath the earth's surface. The water comes from rain and snow that seep through soil into the cracks and other openings in rocks. Groundwater supplies wells and springs.

irrigation: watering land by directing water through canals, ditches, pipes, or sprinklers

open-pit mine: a large hole created to get at metals lying near the earth's surface

prairie: a large area of level or gently rolling grassy land with few trees

precipitation: rain, snow, hail, and other forms of moisture that fall to earth

reclamation: the process of rebuilding land that has been mined and making it usable again for plants, animals, or people

reservation: public land set aside by the government to be used by Native Americans

reservoir: a place where water is collected and stored for later use

treaty: an agreement between two or more groups, usually having to do with peace or trade

INDEX

PHOTO ACKNOWLEDGMENTS

Cover photographs by © David Muench/CORBIS (left) and © Jim Zuckerman/COR-BIS (right); PresentationMaps.com, pp. 1, 8, 9, 49; © Kevin R. Morris/CORBIS, pp. 2–3; © Joel W. Rogers/CORBIS, p. 3; © Stan Osolinski/Root Resources, pp. 4 (detail), 6, 7 (detail), 17 (detail), 41 (detail), 53 (detail); Travel Montana, G. Wiltsie, p. 7; © Alan G. Nelson/Root Resources, p. 10; H. L. James, Montana Bureau of Mines and Geology, p. 12; Montana Power Company, pp. 13, 50; Kent & Donna Dannen, pp. 14 (top), 46, 80; Jerg Kroener, pp. 14 (bottom), 54; © Crystal Images, 1992, Kathleen Marie Menke, pp. 15, 48; Gerry Lemmo, pp. 16, 44; Patrick Cone, pp. 17, 43; © Jonathan Blair/CORBIS, p. 19; Independent Picture Service, pp. 20, 21, 66 (second from top and second from bottom), 67 (top and second from bottom), 69 (second from bottom); The Montana Historical Society, pp. 23, 24, 25 (all), 27, 29, 31, 35, 61, 69 (bottom); United States National Park Service-Warren Collection, p. 28; Library of Congress, pp. 30, 32; The Southwest Museum, Los Angeles (photo #CT.1), p. 33; Chicago Historical Society (negative #11), p. 36; Museum of the Rockies, Montana State University, p. 37; Michael Crummet, pp. 38, 42, 45 (both), 52 (left), 57 (top), 58; Travel Montana, G. Wunderwald, p. 40; Theresa Early, p. 47; Montana Cooperative Extension Service, p. 51; Travel Montana, D. Scott, p. 52 (right); Bryan Liedahl, p. 56; Robin McCulloch, Montana Bureau of Mines and Geology, p. 57 (bottom); Betty Groskin, p. 59; Jack Lindstrom, p. 60; Tim Seeley, pp. 63, 71 (top), 72; Alvina C. Welliver, p. 66 (top); Smithsonian Institution (photo #3405), p. 66 (bottom); Hollywood Book & Poster, p. 67 (second from top); Stuart S. White, Great Falls Tribune, p. 67 (bottom); Stan Paregien, p. 68 (top); Photofest, pp. 68 (second from top), 69 (second from top); Maureen and Mike Mansfield Library, University of Montana, pp. 68 (second from bottom), 69 (top); National Baseball Hall of Fame Museum, p. 68 (bottom); Jean Matheny, p. 70 (top); © Rich Kirchner, p. 73; Travel Montana, Kis, p. 81.